T0162408

KATHLEEN FRASER   m ova b le TYYPE

Also by Kathleen Fraser

Poetry

Change of Address 1966
In Defiance (of the Rains) 1969
Little Notes to You from Lucas Street 1972
What I Want 1974
Magritte Series 1977
New Shoes 1978
Each Next, narratives 1980
Something (even human voices) in the foreground, a lake 1984
Notes preceding trust 1987
when new time folds up 1993
il cuore : the heart / Selected Poems 1970-1995
20th Century 2000
Discrete Categories Forced Into Coupling 2004

Artist books (limited editions)

boundayr [with Sam Francis, aquatints] 1987
from a text [with Mary Ann Hayden, oil encaustics] 1993
WING [with David Marshall, drawings] 1995
hi dde violeth i dde violet [collaged from original Fraser poem] 2003
W I T N E S S [with Nancy Tokar Miller, ink/paint images] 2007
S E C O N D LANGUAGE [collage: text, KF; images JoAnn Ugolini] 2009
ii ss [with Hermine Ford, mixed drawing & watercolor] 2011

Essays

Translating the Unspeakable, Poetry and the Innovative Necessity 2000

For children

Stilts, Somersaults & Headstands [poems based on & illustrated
with Pieter Breughel's "Children Playing Games"] 1968

m ova b le TYYPE KATHLEEN FRASER

Nightboat Books

Callicoon, New York

© 2011 by Kathleen Fraser
All rights reserved
Printed in the United States

ISBN: 978-0-9844598-8-9

Design and typesetting by Kevin Mount
Body text for this edition set in Quadraat; replica of the
Nomados Press printing of hi dde violeth i dde violet
set in Mercury Display

Cataloging-in-publication data is available
From the Library of Congress

Distributed by University Press of New England
One Court Street
Lebanon, NH 03766
www.upne.com

Nightboat Books
Callicoon, New York
www.nightboat.org

Cover Art: "Untitled, n. 16, Rome 2009" by JoAnn Ugolini.
Courtesy of the artist.

for Fanebius Perlyng, ever there,
being the pleasure of my text

Contents

Acknowledgments

Keeping in mind the visual & sometimes unusual typographic content of the Artist Book texts included in this collection, I want particularly to salute those who, with their specific spaces and skills, helped to support the production of these hands-on documents. Abiding gratitude to:

Peter & Meredith Quartermain, Nomados (Vancouver), who asked—sight unseen—for a manuscript to add to their series of works-in-progress and took the challenge when my graphic/ly expanded & unrepentant collaged pages arrived in a file attachment as the book hi dde violeth i dde violet (2004), and to the French poet/translators, Abigail Lang and Omar Berrada, who re-created this work for a bi-lingual audience at the Double Change poetry Series in Paris (2008).

The American Academy in Rome for providing a spacious and beautiful studio for painter JoAnn Ugolini and myself in which to work during April 2009, collaging the images and hand-pasted texts that ended up as the book S E C O N D LANGUAGE. Thanks also to the AAR's library and staff for making available their acquisition of unpublished archaeological research —in particular, one first-century document known as "The Vindolanda Writing Tablets." These field notes, recovered from military bonfire sites in the UK, were recommended to me by Patricia Larish, the Andrew Heiskell Post-Doctoral Fellow in Ancient Studies at the AAR that year. She also lent me her copy of the Latin satirical poet, Martial, whose wit soon found its way into my collaged text...
...and, with particular gratitude to Don Cushman who, as publisher of S E C O N D LANGUAGE [Cloud Marauder Press, Berkeley] designed its codex, accordion-style pages and linen box binding and tirelessly printed —with JoAnn's help—his photographs of our original collages into 15 copies

of the original, overseeing their bindings with two traditional Roman binders at a bottega oscura near the Piazza Navona (Rome).

The Pratt Institute (School of Architecture/Rome) and its curator, Emanuela Ricciardi, for inviting Hermine Ford and myself to hang a show at Pratt (2008) of our open-page texts & drawings—under the title ii ss, preceding their subsequent publication by Granary Books, spring (2011), thus making the work available to an attentive Roman public and Pratt's visiting student artists. Thanks, as well, to Michael Rothenberg whose on-line journal, Big Bridge, n.12, first included some of our early pages as part of a feature on writer-artist collaborations (curated by Vincent Katz).

Publishers Charles Alexander, Chax Press (Tucson), and Steve Clay, Granary (NYC), for taking on the labor-intensive Artist Book projects of W I T N E S S (2007) and ii ss (2011), with a devotion to papers, fonts, bindings and colors not often found. Thanks, too, for their permission to reproduce the original texts from the books they published.

Mille grazie to the Roman poet, Marco Giovenale, for translating W I T N E S S / T E S T I M O N E into Italian and including it in the beautiful chapbook series from La Camera Verde, (2008), under the direction of Giovanni Andrea Semerano

Jeanne Heuving and the staff of The Whitely Center, Friday Harbor Labs (U. of WA), for the invitation and privilege of pursuing work that landed, in part, in the final section of this book as the sequence "What we needed." Jeanne and I worked separately and collaboratively within this Puget Sound community of research scientists, oceanographers and scholar/writers during August of 2007. Four years later—with linguistic, intuitive and visual instincts in close communion—Jeanne read this manuscript culled from ten years of work and gave me the courage to put it into a wider light. For her critical support, I am deeply beholden.

To the co-editors of VERSE, Brian Henry and Andrew Zawacki, who worked tirelessly to complete their first "Portfolio" version of the journal in 2009 (Volume 26, Numbers 1-3) and invited me to select a dossier of work-in-progress, publishing "Ligature, for Mr. Coltrane" and "fisure plural," as part of this selection.

Hazel White, remarkable poet, who provided the second read that only a professional copy editor has eyes for, confirming the presence of yet lurking typos with her delicately put findings. Poets cannot do without such rigorous devotion.

To Kevin Mount, designer of this book, unfailingly patient and willing to consider any idea not necessarily part of the original plan; uncanny reader; detective of my layered intentions; lover of fonts and their more subtle uses, with whom I've been most honored to work—my thanks for all of it, including the grey sans serif.

Finally, to my editor Stephen Motika, rare in this world, who proposed a book that would embrace the seeming contradictions in my work—including a more recent focus on visually foregrounded collaboration with its startling meanings of scale & typography. In prescient ways, Stephen has enabled the process of building this book and has persevered with me in finding its hidden path. He has been the editor one always imagined, hand on the pulse.

20th Century

Orologic

Delay'd the — what was it? — leftover, almost said mainspring
locution — off-putting — lifting's effort of red-wire modest stratagem.

Gem's Spa (Ninth & 2nd) chocolate folio under which egg cream air,
he told you — sutured with tape and geranium rose — his secret

stutterer scrapheap — "...if only we'd...". Said he wasn't spiritual
but could feel the awe — that little Yes material — script pierced (& pierces)

sleep's end of it, rose geranium whistle-stop nape of neck thistle.
Down fallow mind of page — delay'd, early sphere theory.

Margins: Stella begins rebuke: torn shirt Stanley's & white
silent movie-talk ending, a few blue decals

in the projection cabinets. Abuse of reliable matter (embossed),
how "A" connects to its wire. One glance — marron glacé; when

she talks about "frame theory," the game-bird's heartbeat under
glass (fluttery to her as a pamphlet or flock of blank ink), wings tied-off.

Song rebuke rescinds the variable. You often measured
pretense between face and thread, when you demonstrated

linen. Corner understood (unsafe on-camera) reading him:
delay'd erasure, giving him 0 or 1. Syllabic temptation

of yesterday's waving particle. Lawd low Atlantis shallow.
Wrong obsidian lesson & axis ladder & hairpin do not "hold sway."

Kid integer dot picture folds up playground early, witness pulling
her inviolate back a'shine as effacement mirror not seen.

What passed in dark's sidereal cloud chamber festoon'd with giddy
scars is past & perfect. You write "Dear Sir: wherever you be,

please map us there..." (open side of resilient moon yaw

                         — for J. H.

The Disappeared

entablature, missing elements, details
that found the architect's practice

< >

a disappeared part   spirit to doorway's cornice

column of all these unraveled cities

(client more than satisfactory and anyway we are
overwhelmed   useless)

run-after city   all this belonged to us

we walked through the streets arm-in-arm

method: remarking how
in memory the physical world
is not ours

for reflex: a photograph
itself distorts shadow
and real value

.

The studied object at that synthetic level forms in space such as
doorways ... but the noise of radio waves, bottles shattering ...

all those green parrots gone wild
                    (screeking cloud of them hurtling by)

.

Deep signs in the form of our cities' exhausted daily craftsmen never
reached   Silence of the noisy and forced   Houses with littered
causeways   Submerged city roughly put aside with slight regret
Ecstatic tolerance for the shiny missing dead

.

Corner solution, etc.   relatively small &   singled out because it can
be measured   reference to whatever is   visible / axial
digital pencil   laws held at point of disappearing in plastic value   not
merely schematic   Peculiar, for   we can still see   canonical elements
of the classical language   even here, at the point of   disappearance
and   (embellishment) facade techniques   bricked arch   projecting
pilasters' slightly columned attic with hang-out balustrade washing
on line   Egyptian cotton shirts &
hand-cut table linen (old and soft)   the crossed arena yet wide

. . . green parrots loose between buildings . . .

Initially rolling forward
as sculptural coincidence

it evenly astonished us,
this pleasant absent mind

Opposed aristocratic bias,
Stendahlian city moment,

Unitarian re-use
of abusive marbles

"The Rome of the 1931 plan"
close to the ear

---

nest plan : a city as long as a long building

---

molding^   window^   stair^

small lobby cautiously abandoned
unaffordable threshold of a landing never reached

alleys of places (we have lost their names)
so-called baroque time   parrots slashing
through curved light   bent and wrinkled

in the beloved unadorned

— Rome (1995-2000)

A whodunit, for Barbara Guest

Chapter 1

known as a "road murder" list
of three nightdresses tenderly held but
reduced to two by the missing concept

Chapter 2

She: And even as we stood there waiting...
Voice: ... the quicksand began to quiver.

She: You heard the thunder over the sea.
Voice: I saw the see-saw bang against the sea...

She: ...and by chance
Voice: ...the boy crouching for shelter.

She: Solitary?
Voice: A black figure.

She: Among the many, you mean?
Voice: In the physiological dark, I mean.

Chapter 3

Suspicion fell on the sister, on Constance, a girl of a certain age, beneath the anxiety of the dunes, the "else" of sheltering, the lee hard away.

Chapter 4

A: The grandfather, a professional detective...

B: cut on the continental model...

A: within the London Police Force.

B: [rolling his eyes...] Serious, this force!

A: Criminal elements, naturally.

B: The missing garment must bear evidence.

A: You mean "The clue of the missing nightgown"?

B: I read it already, this morning.

A: You've always "already" read it. I did not read it this morning.

B: I found the third nightgown. And there was nothing missing about it...

A: ...though something else?

B: If this were a shut case, Sir, but it is open...

A: Ah, open!

Chapter 5

She was able to produce only two elements
of quicksand's slippery evidence.
Imminent, expecting you
to do something fragrant,
say "Some (other cleaver) lover."

Little gun mare.
Night dream weapon stairs.
The clue of the missing not-
quite-rue (or "full of rue").

She flew high,
white hover in her
missing-few night gown. Now

not quite true.

Chapter 6

still...
expecting something more,
more from the mare of fidelity
outside the ring-fence endowment.
With fragile recompense that skill
irregularly wide at the hover
thereafter plausible
lover's chaste skull-bone and scar

Chapter 7

Reader who supposes
you are the better part of your own
porcelain scandal. A story must be capable,

stabilized in beeswax (rolled cylinder
of heated evening fictional plots), re

solving your six sides
with light at sliced lid.
Light gridlock,

big starry night swerve.

20th Century

1. nor interest in being either

the mother's body not to her own height
a yellow with green with chrome
radiator symmetry anxiety
heated body in parts with
something inconsistent
to heat in the center port
of dependency in which each partition
loves its part, in which
parturition is its height
that which is born, its height
that in the act of its height

.

he more finished
mounted on the surface or base of another
more finished it is
intention to be finished and
to begin

.

she is, nor is she
interested in being either
nor summoned directly into one

into one other, but is
two and dark and richly dark,
dark that is contained in
& next to herself her evasion
geometry brown and black
and rich refusal
that is not beside herself
any particular work

2. *such that qualities of inconsistency*

altered by its
placement the lower half
of her body painted

directly on or against
the surface of a wall
will, in fact, her

studio given
in reward of surface
duress and paint

the black lines meet,
largesse (her
height or private

parts framed
to either) radiator
symmetry

such that qualities
of intent frailty
geometrically

rooted she turning
turns his verticals (law
he made) and said

she loved to break now
corners' directional points
of tablet not

vertical but placed
and painted,
loved,

inconsistent
her private height his
"death of painting,"

arms raised but
inconsistently, but in place
her 20th century

arms, parts
private gendarme stereo
listing, typing

subjecting
"formal weakness"
such that qualities

of frailty
geometrically inconsistent
with any work painted

directly, is drying,
is sure and not
consistent with

finishing
and may change now, is
about to

3. *she explores how any particular work*

is altered by
its placement how any
discrete figure apart
from the bottom half of
its body, where
the legs come together,
or lines representing limbs
of several kinds, though
not attached to a rigor (or
finality) of size, can
utterly collapse

or possibly resuscitate,
can finish or not,
depending upon

the placement of a lighted window
or, in the dark,
an angle where two walls meet
+
if a figure
were in a corner and one saw,
from the distance of an opposite
door, light markings
above the figure, moving
up the angle where two walls
had formed what
an individual mind
might settle upon but
then, moving closer, sees
that what it imagined as
marks are smudges
deposited from air and use
(somewhat indefinite)
that the figure, still being
there, will now have receded,
its impact shifting, while its pure refusal
remains formally intact

how any particular work is altered by its placement how any
discrete figure apart from the bottom half of its body, where the
legs come together, or lines representing limbs of several kinds,
though not attached to a rigor (or finality) of size, can utterly
collapse or possibly resuscitate, can finish or not, depending
upon the placement of windows where two walls meet, if a
figure were in a corner and one saw, from the distance of an
opposite door, light markings above the figure, moving along
the angle where two walls formed what an individual mind
might settle upon but then, moving closer, sees that what it
imagined as marks are smudges deposited from air and use
(somewhat indefinite), that the figure, still being there, will
now have receded, its impact shifting, while its pure refusal
remains formally intact.

—for the painter, Rebecca Quaytman

Alice's shoe

If you look through a magnifying glass, you can get a fair idea of
what she carries in her hand, poised briefly on the metal staircase
pushed up against the body of United Air. Alice, behind her, carries
a small doll in trousers but her hat is elaborate, a kind of printed
turban riding a piece of felt. Alice's shoe, on the topmost step, is
black with a strap across the instep and shows behind Gertrude's
graceful skirt blown sideways by wind.

The photographer has one shot left on this, his first assignment.
He's heard she is a friend of Hemingway's and is taking a chance.
They look tickled pink.

—for D.G.

FOUR ARTIST BOOKS   texts in collaboration

hi dde violeth i dde violet

Dog's body cuts diagonal heav
ing light

coffee melt

forgott—no elite (smell

Collated lilies fallow in
 bakelite shadow shusshing
slippers' advertent pitch
along warm tile amplitudes
 whine of lead pipe's
morning uses. Shutter latc
h creaky bang purrs above
trees' abundant smattering
 lushness. Furry
opened by unseeen hand
light greens. Sharpness of
leaf-crossing-leaf observed

yeasty
   paparazzi
      morning foaling
         still slipping
      guest (rain elides its
naked odors hostess modm)

jammiesSatinpreenSstripes
red
as Greek-dyed Easter egg

fold
    thy   selvesamong
histamine under tongue

smattering

lushness.

Furry

smattering lushness. Fury

waters   all   over   his

pounding host's Sunday

gaseous open door

terroir He breathes bedroom

Air**e** still

brning bittr hrshly

next's

    smell
     in two-way
         Bak
       floor
     noise):

most (&ndles top

—thump thump—

z..." —thump

Radio *linguaggio*

      coming through
      neighbor's hedg
erow

        slice of   nowwhere

                bOther

of

of

offf th

Baze chord windo

skwywr d

him heat hum mind
pieces goat voice fr
m baby pendulum B
iblical teatime tvcut
dth arise to suspend
guest's fine behind tu
cked into   stairs
provoking ginsscent

heeling **&** woofing side-by-their
muzzlels at kitchen door

to side to track surface tension

anything (ears flat back)
to a littll whistll

whereverdog
give listen Our **Lady** hurls

mozzarella in equal prts

up to ceiling'screakybangmetalll**acco**

"What could'a been..."

(ohhh, yeahhhh...)

(oh   **ah**)

ye   ye   **yeh**

ah)   **h)**   ah)**a**

(Vaticano bi-
aggressingthrough

    aggregate   floating

      these molecules' Ceiling
mother)

"He arose!"

"He arrozzz...

thump—(**H**)

a rose...

rose..."

Feeder to herself sing:

from French

door's divided prognostication,

she's noticed panes

damp   hang

hear s

no

o of (fis s **ion**

child-size egg in
hand...or is it already
yesterday?   (belovd,

"Chr   ah"

guests buzzed arise now
& feed &
arrive again with

un observ each gear

b B she'

an urn down
water
risen with

allelujah,

in-laws

rist's

Ch   arisen)
wool socks.

(ears hinged forward

...no longer roll'd awry
inside this any
      thing sliding apart

to greet abi ding

...and tu rn of Ch
other c heek

hidde n

viole nt

h

i

dde

       violeth

          i

        dde

       violet

by unseen hand. Light

opens over trees' abundant

           suspend

Easter / Passover . Rome 2003

WITNESS

rolling against the wall in massive waves so that he should not be one of those

had never—in actuality—been required to know who he was   and to die as
who he had not been

.

Siege in our own cities   can begin to imagine more deeply

one leg ahead

in language under erosion   our trust in corrosive repetition

The airplane entered and entered every wall   The airplane

entered the wall

Up against sure-footedness

or an aspiration   Wanting to rush into silence

I am not ready nor will I be ready to enter the wall of anything that

recommends itself now

The lens hovers   the lens goes out of focus   Now I am back

inside time

All day we sit inside of WAR to the other end

Finally rising with jaw aching   refusing to go forward into

someone's willingness

"I was in school when a voice cracked over the loud-speaker."

The depth of the situation and our on-going willingness not to know

They are trading bomb tonnage statistics, their voices leaking

excitement under the door   She dreams upright from one

end of space that the narrator cut

and fit

fit the historical record to keener dramatic purpose

"I like the feeling of really being frightened," Graves said, with

a dreamy look It will always be there and it will be collapsing

The children's red-knitted shirts seem to hold them up-right something like flags

Collision   "Not a terrorist action."   Meanwhile, I've....

Weighted with news of still being here   and to die as who he had

not yet been

Evidence of breathing   he dreams upright and focused behind

her shut door

Runningfromoneendofspacetotheotherendof s p a c e

Running from the building, leg in air and

we were running, one behind the other, down the same set of stairs

"We had become like wild animals.   We didn't care about anyone other…"

"…but after the next attack, I will help an old man push his basket at the supermarket   He'll say 'Thank you, Sir.' and I will say 'You're very welcome, Sir,' and we'll just go on talking…"

It is always in our peripheral vision

You will always be there and it will be collapsing

SECOND LANGUAGE

in the photo day

summer   machine

Bare feet not school, but the silver
oval was always tall when
we talked them into tiny pin pricks
sinking into oxfords now

See our dry prickly grass as tall
as red leather rain been up, Mom,
just sun outlining the stores.
We are the toes

Day-after-day at
little mud platform
even before bones shining through
in the driveway

"What can we do today, mom?"
She's busy trying late, she

swimm their photo noon
before dressing and plopped us
in that after graph.

Our legs are covered with little
red bites, the

night before the night of
accordion players in the park
who arrive always after supper
with black bumps for different notes

to press when the dark is still good
on one side of walking home.
We run around and follow edges
of trees to make up our own sound

but finally a step is getting thick.
The accordion players squeeze
their pleated boxes out & in
over summer's white paper

and we hear accordion dark
fall into us we've never had.

down   cool green

a jump rope is the curve
in grass and we are thinking
grasshopper music attached
to branches. Our oars are thick

with what we can do still hidden
in the dark scharr ass. We're
husks of dead locusts not here
yet.   But we don't see them

turn from brown to red and then
where do they go above
pinches and tucks of cloth?
The stars find every afternoon.

how in day of flag and

where he was sitting when he
tied oxfords, of first laces
by ourselves yet there.

Was it the morning pulling
new dress over and did we walk
alone, couldn't breathe, didn't

like my woo eyes. When
was the chiggers that brown?

school

The beginning of all I missed
was dying inside my lower lip
from being ice with twigs

as tall as the space between lines
and letters half as turquoise
melted in the photo day.

Anything looks large and still when
something has happened in a pond.
First dead bugs in it, as if it has a

shadow mouth under it, but rounder
and the little bed seems so full
trying to make the big letters

Snow

When I saw the blue tin hole
inside of her lunch
I admired its definite use and

the clean sock preserved in a little
metal stretch pail with no time,

black ink points that no one could
use.

Fluttery in my little brother's
foot show with pink erasers
to twist, not even one of my
pencils with the top she
bought for him

I looked at my wooden measuring.

When did it start being a painted yellow

sharpener feeling marked like arms?

first day.

window shadow
just as grown-ups look into

their passed sheets of
right words

It's the low bumps
song have after

words have

cf. story

Until the 4th century, AD, the book consisted of a length of papyrus attached to rods on which it was rolled.

footnote 2 *Codex*: a Roman invention, gradually replacing the scroll, that first came into use near the end of the 1st century AD with its long accordian-folded strips of papyrus—or vellum *recto verso*—divided into page-size units that could more easily be carried from place to place. The epigrammist, Martial, was the first known to experiment with the codex form for his writings.

from: codex, Wikipedia.org

footnote 3"

: The battle of Lapitas & the Centaurs was painted on the Argo.

+
Monychus was a Centaur;

from Book I:

"The Cilicians" (Sicilians?)

3. "Ah, little do you know
the haughty ways of Lad
Rome! Believe me one more
" ti praestat harena"

reveals Mars' emphatic

children all had noses

Nowhere are sniffs more

emphatic.

after MARTIAL

"Sygambrians have come with hair curled
in a knot and Ethiopians with hair
curled otherwise" & with these
the y found enough patronage
to have an apartment on the Quirinale

up 3 flights of stairs.

[**footnote 8:** of saffron sprin kled over
stage (arena)and spectators' flatteries,
Latin parrots, ravens. Young men, old
men, boys— they be new pieces .
(Cf. "*quidquid Fame, canit*"
... the arena affords you.)]

after MARTIAL: *Epigrams*

but "whatever Fame
signs of"

M. did not take Catullus
as his model of saffron
but courted in genuflective
haughty ways, boys—
on Rome stairs
whose favor he assiduously
turned up his rhino nose at

shaken blanket)

The back is blank.

The writing is obscured by dirt.

<u>P</u> is written with a closed loop (like a capital form

and there is a long   ascending diagonal following

(although   it is not certain to be ink).   The ink

after <u>et</u>   is badly smeared.   The hand is

unremarkable.

From archeological data: SG (bonfire site). Period 5.

435-7 Plate XXV, plate 18

Archeological data. Location: M. Period.

"what survives is the right-hand
half of a diptych, complete at the
foot and the right margin, containing
the second column of a letter,
with an address on the back.... There are
two tie-holes and two v-shaped notches
at the right hand side of the leaf."

435-7 Plate XXV, plate 18

" . . . so that he might send my
money . . . without the knowledge of
his prefect. Greet Vercunda and
Sanctus . . . Capito and all my
fellow countrymen and friends,
with whome I pray that you are in
good health . . . (Back) . . .surveyor
(?),

The sender of the letter was a certain Ascanius

this [....continual erasure]

597 Location: SG bonfire site, Period: 3

"...that the suspended body was known in the Roman world at the end of the first century A.D."

a)...likewise (?) a jointed..(?) Account. From the sheets... for the use (?) of a suspended carriage...

b)...likewise (?) a second bolt for the bread-box, number 1. Repaired pots, number 2.
Dog-collars, number...a bolt (?)...

677, 6. "We are confident that catullum is correct, "meaning a puppy o r a young dog".

The excavation of the 1990s once again produced a significant number of ink texts written on thin wooden leaves.
[   ] stilus tablets <abc> were, as before, omitted

[through spectators]

m1, m2 distinguish different hands in the text
[   ] indicates a lacuna in the text
uacat , a space left by the scribe on the tablet
[[abc]] letters crossed out or erased by the scribe
<abc> letters erroneously omitted by the scribe

[We have made no attempt to..... cross out or erase]

rather fficial function

No. 581
...the decurion(s) of the last beer (?)...

1 March, by Ma . . .
  by Cressons
  . . . . . .
  . . . . . .

30 March, by Mar
31 March, by Exsomnius (?) . . .
  on the same day, by Candidus (?)
23 April by V. . .
  on the same day, by...
  line deleted
26 April

in charge of the draft animals of Brocchus (?)
a goose...
total, geese . . .
likewise, geese

nursling chicks (?). . .
  chickens

16 May (by?) the brewer
18 May (by?)...
  In the 5th consulship of Trajan
  chickens...

"...without the encumbrances of provisional and partial readings by other scholars in the interim..." [from the Preface]

Tabulae Vindolandenses III

d spl cd v w l

d spl c d v w l

have now been asked to
bear access to the
flush of my own worn through

finally certain claim

of anything being closer to saying

Baze chord windo

skwyw rd

Sulfanilamide

from perfect pitch
thin pain in you
made me love you,

you imagine—page folded
inside its scar, these entirely
backward

flaws of embrace, fugue
being of your unfolding
response to a threat,

coolness folds. No
brain folds touched me
They had to roll out

some other's wet sheets

because you understood,

down the synaptic corridor thicket
how even the human footfall

as it accumulates
negates the pure sound of error

while still not being *in* the former
struggling

word worn parties

I spoon was seeking your
separation of mouth's longitudinal
gaze.   Music was misplaced

every day, stubbornly
its black type, your hand and
left wrist fugal, your deficit

compositional, stepping away
or away from pursuit of place.
"Placing it where

you see it" plural,   veering
into a fixed gaze,   I took more.

expectation's nuance

and perhaps thought
mediates to the wing path
instructs itself
no equals sign
of who *am ready*

Fissure

depth. Fissure inherent in
duration but the structure of
fissure
narrow chasm

relocates "true" over-lapping

second language

from laying down
the bend of certainty
you sound [dwell] in one
word enough

resistant to a fact that can
refuse fumbling

ii SS

ii ss : to be

Amphibians are facing a dire global extinction crisis that crystallizes
the impact humans are having on the entire natural world.
—Claude Gascon, *Conservation International*

In April of 2006, soon after this statement appeared in the press, scientists
discovered a fossil on Ellesmere Island in the Canadian Arctic that provided
evidence for the sought-after "missing link" between sea creatures and the
first land-roaming animal ... something approaching a first-stage amphibian.
The struggle involved in making this journey through time and the elements,
from fins to paws, felt extremely urgent—even intimate—although separated
from us by 375 million years.

About to begin a collaborative series in Rome in April of 2006, we had both
been particularly compelled by the visual patterns and alphabets embedded in
the stones, antiquities, mosaics, constellation graphics and fabrics of Indo-
European cultures and had begun exploratory work piecing together these
iconic fragments in our own texts and drawings. But when the "missing link"
fossil appeared, the direction for our project amplified. To be at this end of a
disappearing species, just as its earliest beginnings were discovered, was cause
for alarm and overwhelming sadness.

Yet as we worked, the subject often took its own direction towards celebration
of evolution's unstoppable force—its languages and visual pathways,
continuously reanimated.

ii ss addresses the double-bind of to be—being human and being dependent
upon the natural world for pleasure and sustenance. In this knowledge we
have been awakened, with a harsh jolt, to earth's gradual melting and shifting
due to man's deliberate avoidance patterns, both greedy and neglectful,
leading us to the careless destruction of our planet home.

Rome, April 3, 2007
from program notes, ii ss exhibit, collaborative works on paper,
by Hermine Ford and Kathleen Fraser. Pratt School of Architecture (2008)

in evidence, as "is"

is drawn in stone

disguised as stone

shallow water Afar

of thickening

ile flottante flotilla few & flicker ile flottante flotilla

few & flicker ile flottante flotilla few

flicker ile flottante flotilla few & flicker ile flottante

flotilla few & flicker flottante flotilla few &

flicker ile flottante flotilla few & flicker **ile flottante**

flotilla **few** **& flicker** ile flottante flotilla few & flicker flotilla few &

flicker ile flottante flotilla few & flicker ile flottante

flotilla few & flicker ile flottante flotilla

flicker ile flottante flotilla few & flicker ile

& flicker few **few** flottante

S[p[l[a[sh]S

S[p[l[a[sh]S

S[p[l[a[sh]S

S[p[l[a[sh]S

a fossil ("good") cuts little

laughs through fog

fast-forwarded fin now

where digits feel urgency,

dryness density and

répétiteur

properties of who, with speech

BED OF OVID'S ION PLURAL FUTURE

TO EXPLAIN MULTI-SPECTRAL IMAGING
WE MUST MAKE A SHORT DIGRESSION
INTO ELECTROMAGNETIC RADIATION
WHICH CAN BE UNDERSTOOD AS WAVES
OF ENERGY TRAVELING THROUGH SPACE.
RADIATION CAN VARY IN ITS INTENSITY
(THAT IS HOW MANY WAVES ARE RECEIVED
OR EMITTED WITH A CERTAIN

MAKING LARGE MARKING

fleet

        floating heel

    Achilles

shrewdly

proto-wrists

proliferate in the

forward land-roaming

(Si ritira(It withdraws(Il s'éclipse

Peche   rouge aztèque   Coquille

perle rose pouter   ocre   magnolia

jauneSyracuse   marron glacé   jade

blau st. trop   blanc lunaire

tombouctou   Indian jaune andalou

vert empire   olive   pois

gris décor   ananas   abricot

rose de siam   rouge listrac

palomba   blue   gris

rose antique   blue limoges

blue profound blue   gobi

clémentine   nocturne   tango

gris tourtercelle   vert crystal

champagne   pamplemousse

To fly your kite: Fold at 2. Then fold 1 and 3 together. Fold again at 4. After fold is in position, crease along vertical bottom lines to form a gentle curve. Attach kite string at 5, 6, 7. To fly your kite: Fold at 2. Then fold 1 and 3 together. Fold again at 4. After fold is in position, crease along vertical bottom lines to form a gentle curve. Attach kite string at 5, 6, 7.

already pressed into brain & lung

already pressed into brain & lung

BUT THAT SPARKY BIRD

KEEPS SHEDDING MUSIC

SURVEILLANCE.surveillance

Selected work 2008-2010

Ligature, for Mr Coltrane

ligature: the structure that in certain type faces joins one letter to the next;
in music, a curved line connecting notes to be sung or played as one phrase.

In the spring of 1965, I opened a copy of *The Village Voice* and read a
notice that John Coltrane and his quartet were playing a gig down in
the low-rent West Village neighborhood where I'd rented a room.
Coltrane was booked for two weeks at The Half Note, a murky but
easy-going jazz club where you could skip the cover at the door if
you sat at the bar. The Half Note was on Hudson St., a few blocks
from the West Side highway running along next to the river where
New Jersey's neon signs flashed from the distant shoreline. If you
stayed next to the buildings on the right side, walking south, you cut
out 10 degrees from the wind chill factor. I was twenty and didn't
have much meat on me, nor fat to give me a little extra to go on.

It still felt like winter to me. I had on those cheap wool gloves with
leather stitched to the palm side and the coat my father had given me
for my trip to the city he'd only dreamed of, along with some of his
printed notes on the history of type design, clearly stamped with the
certainty that N, Y and C had settled the question of where to begin
with an alphabet when you were starting to look for a new type face
in the shiny empty field of the metal plate.

Be-bop was on my mind, the first time I sat at that bar. The musicians were leaning forward on their chairs, wiping down their horns like horse flanks, stretching towards the bar for their drinks or pulled up around the baby grand—on our level, instead of above us on a stage—with a couple of metal music stands scattered like props since no one, it seemed, appeared to pay much attention to the written score. The musicians were there, along with drinking customers at tables closer to the front of the room; when I walked in, two of them were already warming-up—one doing random scales and the other tuning his drums for what turned into a good forty-five minutes before Coltrane sat down. You didn't even see him come in he was so quiet.

For two weeks straight, the quartet played "My Favorite Things" or "A Love Supreme," probably every night I went in there. The first set seemed to be the same as the second. I couldn't figure it out. During the first few nights, I kept waiting for some other tunes. Coltrane wore the same brown suit and pressed white shirt every night I heard him, not too shabby but not meant to please. It was like he didn't want to draw any attention to his body—no hats, no gold jewelry.

Everything was already running between his mind and his hands
when he picked up his horn. By then, he never took his lungs for
granted. No smokes. He was closing in on what might happen once
the music began and that's where he wanted your attention.
I came in the first night with expectations from my years in Bruges
where a few friends at my father's foundry collected American
be-bop records, sort of the way I'd heard American boys hoarded
baseball cards for later trades. I hoarded what be-bop classics I
could get my hands on, when I had a little extra cash, but I didn't
trade. I was like a certain kind of bird that knows what it wants,
with an in-born knowledge of what it is good at finding. But I
couldn't find work in the city and finally my money ran out and I had
to go back home to Bruges where they knew me. I figured I could
earn a living where hand-made type was still in demand.

I listened to Coltrane repeat those two songs at least eight times,
before I headed back down to the docks one night in early May to
board a freighter headed for Ostend, the port closest to Bruges.
I don't know exactly when it happened but I'd begun to hear how
Coltrane was trying to find a new way through the tune each time he

picked up his horn. He was always looking for something more than himself around the next corner ... and the other guys followed close behind. He had his back-up.

There was a kind of reverence in that room, by the time he was into his second set. People, if they needed to talk, kept it brief and low. The waitresses worked by sign language. The bar tender knew his place. I'm not a religious person but sitting through those nights was as close as I've come to what church is supposed to be, as near to leaving my body as anything I'd ever felt.

One night I imagined I could hear Mr. Coltrane thinking into the air and it occurred to me that songs could be like old alphabets, going back and back, and someone with a horn and his own way of thinking in sound could cut an old song out of the air like a new typeface finding its inner balance just at the place where a horn player feels something pulling and suddenly changes keys.

something we needed

firstsight

Subtracting from black, it approaches the middle distance of elephant grey
or the disappearance of assigned pigment. The water's surface

defines two of four dimensions, fire having been relatively accessible above
ground even as the land animals were shut away from their familiar huts.

Most water depth had not been measured until there was none.
We were not told, or was it that we didn't know how to recognize the symptoms

as our brains grew feeble from continuously multiplying facts: oil spill tinned
and marketed. Yet certain parts of the alphabet were discovered

along the low grey wall identified as the horizon: X seemed particularly
poignant, suggesting something we needed.

3 Aug

black suitcase

color arrives, green arrives as a sub-set in collaboration
sun having risen in place, again black suitcase
pulled over bed of needles

the doe turns, glances up at intervals,
leans, nibbles at early soaked grass
haunches markedly slanted inward

at knee joints intended for escape
though still seen through glass door with smaller
replica behind her nibbling, glancing up

at black jeans passing
+
wakened by silence   grey light snagged in tree bark continuous
of what had been called nobility of task before & after you stood there

creep and flow of pattern in genus   evergreen all commas

+

If I woke earlier, that is if for any reason my eyes were prompted to open, it was not "from a dream" but that someone's voice said "morning" as if from outside sleep, not the mechanical command of alarm but inviting me to reassemble and inhabit a body as it leaned across cotton sheets to see clock hands at 7:05 a.m. Some sort of brain scan, J. at the door of sleep, not physical in the normal way one thinks of bodily presence but as in the signal of a passenger ship approaching—you, in unmeasured depth still sleeping, being the harbored one in middle distance. The chromatic balance had again arrived to reassure and with its questions startle the body, grateful to be yet touched by cotton depth, green and blue the medium in which we understood the ship coming closer.

4 Aug

side bar (a kind of arrival

It becomes more difficult to know where to start. Look at your own desk...
cartons filled with bubble-wrap arrive and seem to ignite the progress of
worry. Why bother? is a common thought impeding the process of scanning
and filing.

Only this morning the lab of a research scientist was abandoned to flying
termites. The public believes the pervasive smell of rot that hovers over the
town as they step off the ferry onto protected land is the natural world turning
over on the weekend. We are here. And happy to be here,

to be here,   to be here.

5 Aug

being intermittent

"Proust described 'the intermittences of the heart': someone
should describe the intermittence of being." —Antonin Artaud

singular, to take in fully any aspect of the body without
its cotton t-shirt and sturdy black denims—to think
of his skin just after rising, sex asleep now in its ambient
staggering into darkness—perception of elbow and knee joint
held in stillness as if a mechanical device were perched
to advance the film, one more frame moved forward,
numerically fluent (yet his pulse is electrical
and muscular), stopped intent of metallic aperture

·

you were not on the verge of disappearing or
re-emerging to become a tree, each side of your body
now holding the wished-for rope of descent—possibly,
perilously down the worn stairs to wct sand and piled
driftwood core of cypress trunk with no evident measurable
pulse, storm-washed, drained of mineral, the stain
plowed under, under

but you were waiting for something fully formed that
in side-step would alert you, pull you to its intermittent claim on you,
this rescuing being a rendering-up of today's shed margin.

7 Aug

empty . sea . in . mind

In empty expectancy, what movement may reveal itself stepping from behind the cypress sending signals out to its planetary rings—furthest ring closest to bark already peeling—taking on cell mass, porosity in which chambers swiftly constructed now lean in to gather moisture, even in error.

.

Edge of scraped skin peeling back under pressure of cellular arrival, intermittent light having equal periods of shining and eclipse. Wave periodicity. We are at our desks. Tiny lamps shine back at us from early fishing boats scooting over the Sound's icy water; now gearing forward, the boats clip trails of white left behind as they surge ahead.

Foam and scum pools gather near shore; if this is run-off, the salty days are leaving us. What happens to the formal holding place of each born thing when its shape dissolves to liquid?

.

Waking alert, ear cones shifting position—weight of insect tipping over tinfoil scrap (walking in place, wanting any bird to hop and skitter).

A willingness to choose evaporation, remote from land as ice is to the saltiest part, polar seas continuously entering

mosquito's delicate leg joints as it lands on your arm, seeking blood.

.

Remoteness is salt. What water leaves behind will be added or subtracted in rapid degrees of separation—the urgency to crystallize and shine, as decisions wait in all of us.

Animals suddenly there on the other side of glass, resolute with their intelligence-gathering spread evenly through the body. Factual tactility, tenacious weed attached to wood frame leaking stain as if to ground itself.

You wake up to throbbing, scanning for memory of an injury whose incipient arrival cannot be seen, as if secluded in its own band-width.

8 Aug

a photo is often identified

1.
A photo is often identified incorrectly. Americans in an apartment building several blocks away, seen from here, are trying to climb a ladder to board the helicopter sent for them after the war of boundaries has been earmarked but legally prohibited at ground level until the 10 meter level is reached as indicated by a thin red line.

In the jewel heist cluster, the police department's all-points search finally leads to the 2 star Hotel Utrillo in that neighborhood of Paris notorious for its sex shops and red light district, where known suspects Mr. V. and Nikola I. stand as if unmoving, unable to stop touching their Swiss-made Patek Phillippe watches, these particular models the very ones exchanged by figures of Italian nobility and their well-wishers during the passing back and forth of ceremonial wedding contracts between the bride and groom's family lawyers whose white cuffs provide an arena for discrete left & right-handed timepieces, watches being so much easier to copy than diamonds.

One of the two has hidden a blue diamond in a jar of face cream just as he's seen them do in a famous jewel heist movie from when he was a boy. On the evening news, thieves have struck a shop in Monte Carlo and investigators remain baffled by the get-away car of choice, the thieves escaping in a yellow Fiat, finally abandoning it yet leaving inside it their fingerprints to confuse the alibi with a crowd surge.

Happiness, though, is a stubborn emotion to convey in prose. In ancestor healing, you inherit a family member's unfinished business. Each night, food is taken from the supper table directly to the grandparents' burial place. In the baby section of one Tokyo cemetery, all the gravestones have faded red bibs hanging down their fronts as if waiting for soup. It is hard not to look at them and understand that soon the crows will dive down for any bits of food that remain.

2.

After the Aquila earthquake, the Vatican's second highest official tells a crowd of local mourners: "Death teaches us that everything can stop in a moment. When everything ends, all that remains is love"…also stray dogs, abandoned suitcases, looters, envy of those with still-standing houses. Rows of fold-up cots remain, each with its ink-marked blanket, and rumors of shoddy building practices by mafia contract. No empty water bottle remains, nor a random act's exact feeling.

+

Heat path, positions of enzymes. Curdled lead. The heavy, star-flecked pages. Enough time to do its job properly. Giving way under one's own weight to evoke entropic pressure. Gravity cooperates. The police and fire crews assemble as one photo-image for the still existent citizens.

fissure plural,

fugal, your deficit and prize in another's unfold;

or relocates "true" pain without seeking your permission—

as a thin pain in your left wrist will stubbornly remain

.

in its response to a threat, the fissure you imagine—

page folded backward from black type. The brain folds

a fixed gaze, may stray into fog or away from the withheld

.

that made me love you more. I took your hand and mis-

placed it in pursuit of "placing it where I could finally see it"—

deep separation of frontal lobe's fugal error

.

always probing some other's gaze. Music was (is) depth,

a true vein in the rock you are backing into.

Fissure equals the chasm of your mouth's clean longitudinal

.

embrace, its flaw inherent in the brain's connected folds.

Not about cure. It has the structure of overlapping duration

but the fugue, being a compositional device, is

.

contiguous. Stepping away from perfect pitch

pulls silence around you. You sing

"I acknowledge the plurality"—as if talking to yourself.

Il Gatto dell'Etna

An Italian story

There was an orange in the box of oranges. It was wrapped in tissue paper imprinted with a red square, a black circle and a green tree of overlapping leaves hiding even smaller ivory blossoms ... all this under a sky called azurro or French blu (the same sky).

It was 7 o'clock in the evening and il Gatto dell'Etna stood nervously on the dark green grass inside the black circle guarding a perfect orange that lay before him in the grass. His whiskers were as quiet as wire.

He was looking slightly worried, as if another animal or a person might suddenly appear—someone larger, who wanted the orange and would reach for it.

Il Gatto dell'Etna could hear the red square thinking: "I need more red."

In a nearby room, the others ate their pears.

.

Q: "Scelte dalla bellezza naturale superiore alla Natura?"
A: Choices beauty makes are in the mind of the beholder.

holding beauty : being beauty

..."the bee-loud glade" an Irish idea of the beautiful

.

sting = stung

Only 6 sides to every story, repeated the Queen
...no further incursions, please, into the hexagon enclave!

(A model wherein natural selection & nobility both wanted representation.)

.

Domenichino's study of the male figure in which a man's right foot breaks
through the passe-partout and beyond the frame ... thrilling to a woman
gazing from just barely inside the twenty-first century.

or Bellori's "piccolo gabinetto"

: the little cupboard unfolded into glass shelves in a yellow room on the second floor of the Palazzo delle Esposizioni, chosen by the Director and her committee, meant to set aside (to elevate?) Bellori's own particular choices from hers/theirs. His beauty now their idea of his idea. Ours.

.

Ero e Leandro, as Rubens paints them. Actual women overwhelmed by waves, real bodies sliding perilously vertical. The shock of ferocious properties, water in combat with creatures meant for land.

.

"I could never mirror nature. I would like to paint what it leaves me with."

.

coma   comet
hesitant to name his intent to pounce

.

Rooms according to the position of the sun in different seasons, the pears remaining in the fruit bowl. We peel off their harsh green skins and the juice begins to glisten on our thumbs.

.

Il Gatto dell'Etna remains watchful. The red orange just at his feet seems to have tilted in the evening light. His tail breaks the frame of the black circle. His eyes refuse to be tamed by false ideas.

.

Caught in the act of hanging freshly washed curtains, a thought comes to the observing one: "I, too, noted and was struck by the 'ruby satellite' metaphor of the red orange."

In the market, the oranges long for their tissue coverings.

Il gatto dell'Etna [The cat from Etna] is the brand name of a Sicilian blood orange.
+
"I could never mirror nature..." —Joan Mitchell

Notes

20th Century

Orologic

from "*orologio*" —in Italian meaning timepiece or wrist watch—the title
proposes a particular time frame for entering memory-life, NYC mid '60s /
Lower East Side, a new inside-out hybrid—the potential plasticity of language
heightened by its transfusion from new push-back urban energies delivered via
paint, dance and music specifically American-made as in John Coltrane, John
Cage, Yvonne Rainer, Joe Brainard, Joan Mitchell. Known in harsh public
sidewalk light, sentences dangled in one's ear of such surprise you could only
seek the solitude of your journal and try to break the code. Re-setting your wrist-
watch.

20th Century

written for the painter Rebecca Quaytman, spring 2000, after visiting her Rome
studio and looking at hesitancy become physical—her first marks on unmarked
walls, emerging from the corners and proportions of that seemingly vast
"empty" work space. Talking, writer-to-painter. Her shifting assumptions
allowing the reception of a new scale and tilt—how the room turned her away
from certainty to instruct her, pull her inward, wayward.

First published in the a+bend chapbook series (SF) curated by Jill Stengel, in
which authors were introduced to the hands-on production of their own books
by inviting each writer to select cover stock, papers, colors and fonts for his/her
book design. Quaytman's painting is on the cover of 20th Century—a black-on-
gray reproduction substituting for the bottle-green ovals and hay-colored field
of the original.

Four Artist Books, texts in collaboration

hi dde violeth i dde violet
begun as a somewhat traditional narrative description of Pasqua and
Pasquetta—Easter & the day after, celebrated every year by Romans in the
countryside. The intention was to capture my "movie" of such a weekend in
2004—within the happy confines of one particular extended family—a notation
of certain cultural differences I hoped would amuse my poet friend Norma,
who'd recently suffered a stroke and had not yet recovered her ability to speak.
Writing from the impossible position of saying something real that might
acknowledge her situation yet possibly amuse her, I came to an impasse—
worked-over drafts of a condensed, highly polished poem that finally felt
completely beside-the-point. I gave up and filed it away.

Some weeks later, four artist friends—in the middle of hanging a show—invited
me to participate in their opening by giving a reading. Their inclusion of me,
while appreciated, seemed outside the terms of the oil & canvas event. But it did
put me in touch with my frustrated desire to make more hands-on work, further
extending the graphics of typography in my work, visual "intrusions" having
shown up in my poems over the years. I woke up one morning knowing how I
would re/make the poem for Norma by foregrounding the material aspect of the
Pasqua text —enlarging it, cutting it apart and making wall pieces from it. Not
for the show, but for the pleasure of re/finding the meanings which had
compelled me on a scale of arbitrariness.

I worked non-stop, using every word, letter and punctuation mark in the
original and static text. This meant doubling-up on some vowels or consonants
and allowing intentional misspellings, the product of which quickly absorbed
me in its inventive possibilities. I ended up with 31 texts that I hung—happily—
along one wall of my study and invited an audience of 2 to "view".

Quite by chance, within weeks, I received an email from Peter & Meredith Quartermain (Vancouver) asking if I might have a smallish size manuscript available for them to include in their Nomados series. I reformatted the wall pieces to their suggested page size and sent the manuscript on its way.

WITNESS

comes from journal pages kept during the days & weeks immediately following the 9/11 attacks. This tracking became a daily ritual of necessary acquaintance, noting with a kind of microscopic scrutiny the small behaviors of those in my ordinary San Francisco life, distanced from the East coast but trying to absorb through endless repetition of narrative, via TV footage and fragmented speech, facts of the once unimaginable.

The selected text was first written in collaboration with Spanish painter, Gonzalo Tena, for his Maeght Gallery triptych series (2001-2002 / Barcelona), subsequently published in VOLT, n.13, "The WAR issue". In 2006-07, Chax Press (Tucson), published that same text as a limited edition Artist Book, paired with ink/ pastel drawings and linoleum prints, made in specific response by Nancy Tokar Miller.

SECOND LANGUAGE

began when a poem of mine was paired with an intaglio line drawing by JoAnn Ugolini (then unknown to me) for a show of broadsides curated by Kathy Walkup in conjunction with an ED/HD conference at Stanford (late Seventies) featuring Bay Area women printers, poets and visual artists. By the mid-eighties we'd become friends and she'd drawn the cover art for my Kelsey St. book *Something (even human voices) in the foreground, a lake* and we'd both begun spending every spring in Rome (Trastevere) with our writer husbands, the four of us often meeting to exchange new work.

At some point, JoAnn began focusing almost exclusively on collage, working directly from old political posters peeled from Rome walls after rain loosened them. I also wanted to work with collage procedures, but was interested in typography—and SCALE—the difference these made in the perception of a text. We applied for a Visiting Artist's studio grant at the American Academy in Rome to collage a book, proposing the material elements of historic and contemporary Italian culture, randomly chosen, as well as pre-language childhood memories.

With one month's use of a light-filled studio, we worked for long hours every day and completed a three-part book, collaged from graphics found and re/composed using both recent urban and archaeological sources, and finished in time for a studio show of S E C O N D LANGUAGE. In May, the codex form of our book was "bound" by Roman binders in a traditional tied linen box.

ii ss
texts from the recent collaboration with painter Hermine Ford's mixed media drawings, emailed (with pdf.s) back & forth, over a year's time, as a call & response document, answering-on-arrival the next phrase in the conversation. Intended as an Artist Book, the pairs of open-book pages were first exhibited at the Pratt Institute for Architecture in Rome (2008), later bound into the completed letter press book published by Granary (2011), recently shown at the Codex International Book Fair.

Surveillance.surveillance
selected prose works and poems written in between the collaborative Artist Books and chapbooks collected here.

About Kathleen Fraser

Since the publication of *Change of Address* in 1966, Kathleen Fraser has published fourteen poetry collections and seven limited-edition artist books in collaboration with American painters, as well as a book of essays, *Translating the Unspeakable: Poetry and the Innovative Necessity* (2000). Her poetry collections include *New Shoes* (1978), *Something (even human voices) in the foreground, a lake* (1984), *il cuore : the heart, Selected Poems, 1970-1995* (1997) and *Discreet Categories Forced Into Coupling* (2004). In 1987, Fraser was invited by the painter Sam Francis to collaborate on an artist book, *boundayr*, after her poem of that name. Since then, she's worked with five more American artists. The most recent collaboration *ii ss* was written over a year of long-distance exchanges with painter Hermine Ford and published in 2011. For more than four decades, Fraser has lived in San Francisco, where she taught as a professor of Creative Writing, directed The Poetry Center, and founded The American Poetry Archives at San Francisco State University. In the early 1980s, she co-founded and edited the journal *HOW(ever)*, focused on the poetry of innovative contemporary women and scholarship restoring the great works of modernist women writers. Fraser has been the recipient of the Frank O'Hara Poetry Prize, two N.E.A. Poetry Fellowships and a Guggenheim Fellowship in Poetry that took her to Italy in 1981, unexpectedly turning her into a part-time resident of Rome, where she lives every spring with her philosopher/translator husband, Arthur Bierman.

photo: Jeannette Montgomery Barron

Nightboat Books, a nonprofit organization, seeks to develop
audiences for writers whose work resists convention and transcends
boundaries. We publish books rich with poignancy, intelligence and
risk. Please visit our website, **www.nightboat.org**, to learn more
about us and how you can support our future publications.

This book was made possible by a grant from the Topanga Fund,
which is dedicated to promoting the arts and literature of California.

In addition, this book has been made possible, in part, by a grant
from the New York State Council on the Arts Literature Program.

NYSCA